STRATEGIC PLANNING

A Roadmap to Success for Your Organization

DEBRA VINSON

ENDORSEMENT

If you're looking to grow, establish or reposition your organization for greater success, then I highly recommend Debra Vinson's *Strategic Planning: A Roadmap to Success for Your Organization*. Debra's extensive professional experience, educational background and passion for helping organization's create a structure for success, is evident throughout this book as she gives step-by-step guidelines, as well as pitfalls to avoid, when developing and executing your organization's strategic plan.

Apostle Ron Wilson
Senior Pastor, Full Gospel Christian Assemblies Int'l

First Edition: January 2017

10 9 8 7 6 5 4 3 2

CONTENTS

FOREWORD

Distinct determination, are the words any organization to achieve their business goals, success objectives and financial endeavors.

Visionaries see the projected outcome in their minds, and it is imperative that fundamental steps are in place to help initiate a company's progress. This is most assuredly a precious commodity that needs to be considered for any business market in today's time. The manual *Strategic Planning: A Roadmap* to success is such a catalyst to convey this informative task.

Pastor Dave White
Executive Administrator, Day-to-Day Operations
Full Gospel Christian Assemblies International

FOREWORD

While in the contemplative stage of setting up a Strategic Plan, it is important that you are able to provide an overview from the key stakeholders. It is very difficult to understand and promote what you cannot visualize. Most plans fail to get off the ground because the vision from the top was not clear for take-off. Within this book, Debra Vinson has identified key components to help organizations understand strategizing, implementation and execution of a strategic plan.

The key components in preparing a strategic plan should   start with:

- Mission-Organization Purpose
- Vision-Drives Organizations Actions
- CoreValues-Organizaiton Advances Organizations Goals and Objectives

Debra will help you to establish the baseline for identification of these three standards critical to moving forward with your strategic plan. There are so many variables that are inclusive to the plan; however, once we lay the foundation for the plan there are other components that help in closing the deal.

It is not enough to just put words on the paper and proclaim, it is finished and done. This is where we fail. We have a document that becomes a guiding force, but it has no wind. How do we get from Point A to Point B?

- Execution-Development, Education and Adjustment
- Implementation-Plan the Work and Work the Plan

Make sure that there is engagement by all stakeholders-board, senior leadership, management and most critical, your frontline workers who are the organization's ambassadors. You should also have consistent messages that allow you to make adjustments, as noted by the writer, if it is not meeting the needs of the organization and benchmark where you are in the plan, as well as where your competitors are in relationship to your plan. Knowing where they are in relationship to you will help you to measure your success. When you begin to implement the plan all systems are go, now you can begin to plan your work and work your plan. Work, plan and work, this is where you move your organization's operations. This body of work is your organizations Strategic Operations Manual.

Brenda K. Mitchell, BA, MBAExecutive Leadership Professional

INTRODUCTION

"When it is obvious that the goals cannot be reached, do not adjust the goals, adjust the action steps" - Confucius

I wrote Strategic Planning: A Roadmap to Success for Your Organization because I enjoy seeing organizations stand for decades and become great leaders within their respective industry. Far too often, both small and large organizations fail either because they don't have a strategic plan in place, or their plan has not been updated since they initially created it. I hope this book on strategic planning has what you or your organization is looking for and that it helps you to move forward as a winning organization.

" Good business leaders create a vision, articulate the vision, passionately own the vision, and relentlessly drive it to completion."

- Jack Welch

CHAPTER ONE

Strategic Planning:

A strategy is defined as a high level plan to achieve one or more goals under conditions of uncertainty. Any organization that aims to be successful must have a strategy in place that will aid them in achieving their goals and objectives.

While having a strategic plan creates a roadmap that will help lead your organization in the direction you desire to go, implementing one will help your organization to operate more effectively.

There are statistics that have shown that more companies fail because there was not an effective plan put in place. If you want your organization to move forward you cannot shoot from the hip. The plan must be clear and concise. In creating a strategic plan you must have insight and foresight.

Insight: an instance of apprehending the true nature of a thing, especially through intuitive understanding; penetrating mental vision or discernment; faculty of seeing into the inner character or underlying truth.

Synonyms- understanding of, appreciation of, revelation.

Foresight: the ability to predict or the action of predicting what will happen or be needed in the future.

Synonyms – forethought, planning, farsightedness, vision, anticipation, prudence, care, caution, precaution, readiness, preparedness.

Creating a strategic plan may involve 24/7 work. It has been reported that 15 percent of organizations around the world have reported that they are successful at strategy implementation (ibid). Other studies have reported that the implementation of strategic planning failure rate is 60 to 90 percent (Kaplan & Norton, 2005). What this means is that organization's have been successful at developing a strategic plan, but failed when actually implementing or executing the plan. To avoid this pitfall, and increase the success of your execution, write the steps for executing your strategy into your plan. Note obstacles that may arise, and provide potential solutions. In other words, create both a Plan A and a Plan B; and always remember that it's good to have some type of plan, rather than no plan at all.

" Strategy without tactics is the slowest route to victory. Tactics without strategy is the noise before defeat. "

- Sun Tzu

Benefits of having a strategic plan include:

- **It gives direction.** Strategic planning gives you clear directions, which will ultimately help those involved in the execution of your organization's strategic plan to stay commtted and focused on the organization's goals and objectives. Direction brings clear guidance.

- **It gives you the ability to make better business decisions for your organization.** Strategic planning gives you the ability to make business decisions that are beneficial for the success of the organization and can help you have a competitive advange within your the industry.

- **It increases job satisfaction among employees.** Increasing job satisfaction among employees will help you maintain a low employee turnover, retain your best employees and create a better workplace.

- **It helps with the overall financial planning of the organization, and with improving profitability and market share.** Having a strategic plan helps with the overall financial stability of the organization for both market share and shareholders.

While it's important to know the benefits of having a strategic plan, you must also understand why strategic plans fail, so that you can avoid these pitfalls when developing your strategy. According to Cascade, a leading strategy development company, there are seven main reasons that strategic plans fail.

The top seven reasons that strategic plans fail include:

Unclear Objectives- It's not enough to know what results you'd like to see, you must also know what steps you are going to take to achieve those results. Your objective should be clear and to the point. Your strategic plan should be created in such a way, that the actions to be taken are clear and obvious.

Lack of buy-in from your team- Whether you have a team of 5 or 50, it is essential to have buy-in from the entire team. Why? Because your team are the hands and feet of your strategy; and getting the right information and feedback from them, and permitting them to contribute will empower them to buy-in. They are the ones who will help in the execution of the plan. If you don't have buy-in from them, your plan will probably fail because you don't have adequate support.

Lack of Alignment- Everyone on your team should have an understanding of how their individual goals and tasks align with the strategic plan at hand. In your meetings, make sure they are all are on the same page as you.

Failure to account for business as usual-As you execute a new strategy, it is equally important to consider your current business. It's important to have a strong leader who can effectively manage existing business so that this portion of your operation does not fail.

Loss of Momentum- Most people are extremely optimistic and enthusiastic in the initial development stages of their strategic plan. However, somewhere in the middle of development and execution, that enthusiasm wanes or comes to a complete stop. To maintain momentum and a sense of excitement, do the following:

- Have daily or weekly meetings; and
- Use strategic words within your meetings like plan, strategic, goals, objectives ideas, etc. Ensure that your strategic plan is always at the forefront of your team member's minds.

Unwillingness to Iterate- Smart leaders constantly have their ear to the ground; listening for threats and opportunities and moving quickly to adjust plans as needed. Though pivoting and making adjustments may be necessary, you should avoid shifting directions too many times as this may cause you to lose the credibility with your team members. Before you make any changes, think the change through carefully, and weigh all factors.

Failure to Celebrate Success- Often times leaders just talk about the failures of their team, and at times the highlight is mostly on this area. However, celebrating success usually results in more success. Show appreciation by praising and celebrating your team members for their hard work. It is important to celebrate milestones. Celebrating success allows you to show your team members that you could have not done it without them. When you celebrate your team it is important that you talk about what they have done to make to move the organization closer to its goals and objectives. Celebrating success is also a way to help in boosting the morale of the organization.

Exercise

Please list areas where you believe you can improve your strategic planning?

_____

_____

_____

_____

_____

_____

_____

_____

_____

_____

How soon will you implement the changes?

_____

_____

_____

_____

_____

What do you think will happen when you implement the changes?

_____

_____

_____

_____

_____

_____

_____

Are you ready to develop a strategic plan that will move your organization forward. As you move throughout this book, you will find a model that you and your organization can use to develop a strategic plan and reach your desired goals and objectives.

Mission Statement:

One of the key components to crafting a strategic plan is formulating an organizational mission statement. The mission statement should state the purpose, philosophy and overall goals of the organization. Every member of the organization must understand and apply the mission statement if your organization is to be successful.

What is it that you do? The mission statement should clearly communicate your organizational purpose in a concise matter. Those who read your statement should understand your purpose and your philosophy. When you create your mission statement, those that read it can feel your passion about what you do and what you value.

Vision:

It is important that you have a clear vision for your organization. Your vision statement is the road map that will keep you focused on your organizational goals and objectives. Knowing what your organization wants and desires to achieve, will help guide the decision making process and drive your actions.

Exercise

What is your mission statement?

_____
_____
_____
_____
_____
_____
_____

Think about the vision you have for your organization. What is it that you would ultimately like to achieve?

_____
_____
_____
_____
_____
_____

Write your vision statement.

_____
_____
_____
_____
_____
_____
_____

What are your organization's goals and objectives?

_____
_____
_____
_____
_____
_____
_____
_____
_____
_____
_____
_____
_____
_____
_____
_____
_____
_____
_____
_____
_____
_____
_____
_____
_____
_____
_____
_____
_____
_____
_____

" Determine what behaviors and beliefs you value as a company, and have everyone live true to them. These behaviors and beliefs should be so essential to your core, that you don't even think of it as culture."

- Brittany Forsyth, VP of HR, Shopify

CHAPTER TWO

Core Values:

In the beginning of the planning process, it's important to identify your organization's core values. Core values are principles that dictate behaviors and guide actions. Having them in place will help you to measure whether or not your organization is moving in the right direction to achieve its goals. It will also help to measure staff performance and contributions in advancing your organizational goals and objectives.

Exercise

What are your organization's core values?

_____
_____
_____
_____
_____
_____
_____
_____
_____
_____
_____
_____
_____
_____
_____
_____
_____
_____
_____
_____
_____
_____
_____
_____
_____
_____
_____
_____

The Decision Makers in Your Organization:

When developing your strategic plan, it is important that you know who the decision makers are for your organization. There are decision makers at every level of your organization. At the corporate level are VP's, CEO's and Board of Directors. At this level, the decision makers are concerned with both financial and non-financial goals, shareholders, competitiveness, the organization's reputation and the organization's future. Outside of this level, you have the middle managers also known as the center

leaders of the organization. Middle Managers must be capable of translating the decisions made on the corporate level to other divisions within the organization. Next, you have the lower rung of decision makers. This level is made up of managers who work with production, performance, human relations, accounting and marketing, and help to carry out decisions made by the top tiers of leadership. At this level, it is very important that you have the right people in place, as they are the actual implementers of the goals outlined.

Regardless of the level an individual occupies within the decision making process, all staff must be committed and loyal, and in agreement with what the organization is seeking to accomplish. Involving employees at varying levels of leadership within the decision-making process is another tool that can be used to improve production and performance, and increase employee morale.

Exercise

List the decision makers in your organization, and the role they will plan in developing and/or executing your strategic plan?

_____
_____
_____
_____
_____
_____
_____
_____
_____
_____
_____
_____
_____

Are there some roles that still need to be filled? List those roles.

_____
_____
_____
_____
_____
_____

Hiring Process:

The human resources department is a vital part of the organization. The human resources department must be in full support of the organization. The tactics they employ during

the hiring process must align with company goals and objectives.

The functions of the human resource department include:

- Recruitment

- Compensation and Benefits

- Procedures & Policies

- Safety within the Organization

- Compliance

- Training and Development

- Employee Relations

Corporate Social Responsibility and Business Ethics

Organizations have a social responsibility to be ethical both socially and in business. Being ethical in both of these realms is called CSR (Corporate Social Responsibility). There are different types of CSR:

- Economic Responsibility
- Legal Responsibility
- Ethical Responsibility

Having the Right Staff Members in the Right Place

Having the right people in the right positions will help an organization to be successful in reaching its goals. It is important that your staff have the right skills, knowledge and experience so that they can do their jobs effectively. However, you should not stop there. Your staff members should also exhibit characteristics that indicate they can fit within the culture of the organization.

In order to determine whether or not someone is a good fit for your organization, the hiring manager must know what to look for.

Hiring managers should look for:

- Skilled people
- Knowledgeable people
- Experienced people
- People who fit in with the culture of the company

- People who can take directions
- People with social intelligence
- Their Online Reputation (View their Social Media Presence)
- Nepotism

" Building a visionary company requires one percent vision and 99 percent alignment."
- Jim Collins and Jerry Porras

3

CHAPTER THREE

Execute the Strategic Plan

For many people it is easy to write the plan, but the most difficult part is actually executing it. Fortunately, there are steps, as you will see outlined below, that can be taken to ease the implementation process and aid an organization in executing their outlined plan.

As you begin to implement your strategic plan, it is important to note that you may have to make adjustments when you see that your current plan or certain components within your plan are not working. Failure to alter your plan when necessary may cause the organization to fold.

When executing your strategic plan, the following things

should be considered.

1.) The plan must first be developed.

2.) Have the right people in place (management and employees).

3.) Effectively communicate. Communication is essential and you should have the right information, producers and policies in place to ensure your message is being properly conveyed.

4.) Create realistic goals and objectives so that you can stay on course.

5.) Monitor your plan through tracking and reporting.

6.) Determine your short and long term objectives.

7.) Performance Management. Evaluate your staff, know what they are doing, make them accountable and reward them when necessary.

8.) Make sure all staff has the necessary tools to accomplish the responsibilities they have been assigned (technology, information and data, etc.).

9.) Involve your employees in the decision-making process.

Back-up Plan

In developing your organization's strategic plan, you should also develop a back-up plan just in case something in your initial strategy goes awry. Having a back-up plan in place can help your organization to save both time and money, and minimize the impact of whatever did not initially work out.

" However beautiful the strategy, you should occasionally look at the results."
- Sir Winston Churchill

CHAPTER FOUR

SWOT Analysis

To monitor the success of your organization it is important to conduct a SWOT Analysis, which will give you an overview of where the organization is internally and externally.

SWOT broken down is:

S-Strengths- What are the strengths of the organization internally? What are the strengths of the organization in comparison to competitors within the industry?

W-Weaknesses- Are there any deficiencies within the organization? How do those deficiencies (weaknesses) compare to the competition?

O-Opportunities- What areas within the organization need improvement? Areas of improvement may include: change of management, technology, relationships, supplies, etc.

T-Threats- Are there any internal or external threats? Organizations may experience threats as new competitors arise or new technologies are implemented. To counter threats and remain competitive, an organization may need to acquire new resources.

Benchmarking

Your organization should be concerned with benchmarking. Benchmarking is how the organization measures themselves against other organizations within the same industry. Typically when benchmarking, an organization will measure their corporate strategies against that of their competition. This process will reveal where improvements are needed.

Employee Satisfaction

Employee satisfaction helps with the stability of an organization. When you have employees who know that their employer is as concerned about their needs, as they are concerned about the goals of the organization, you will have more committed employees. Employee Satisfaction improves performance, productivity, attendance, trust and loyalty. General recognition and implementation of incentives can help to ensure employee satisfaction and bring growth to the organization.

Exercise

List your organization's strengths.

_____
_____
_____
_____
_____
_____
_____
_____
_____
_____
_____
_____
_____
_____
_____
_____
_____
_____
_____
_____

List your organization's weaknesses.

_____
_____
_____
_____
_____
_____
_____

_____

_____
_____
_____
_____
_____
_____
_____
_____
_____

List the opportunities that exist for your organization.

_____
_____
_____
_____
_____
_____
_____
_____
_____
_____

List your organization's internal and/or external threats?

_____
_____
_____
_____
_____
_____
_____
_____

" You've got to think about big things while you're doing small things, so that all the small things go in the right direction."
-Alvin Toffler

CHAPTER FIVE

Financial Analysis

The financial health of an organization must be monitored on a consistent basis. Assessment is a must. Organizations should focus on income statements, balance sheets and cash flow statements, so that they are aware of where money is going, and if necessary, know where it should be shifted in an effort to achieve company goals and objectives. Adequately monitoring the financial accounting of an organization, will also aid you in being aware of the misappropriation of funds, should the issue arise.

Invest In Your Employees

It is extremely important that leaders invest in their employees. One way to invest in employees is to ensure that they get continual training and development, make sure benefits and compensation align with with the industry salary base, hire the best candidates for the position who also exhibit characteristics in line with with the company culture, and implement initiatives that keep the morale of the employees high. All these things will help employees to be loyal and aid in improving employee retention.

Implement and Work It

The implementation of your strategic plan will take work. You must stay faithful in your application in order to see the results you desire. You must work daily to meet your goals and objectives. **IT TAKES WORK!** You must walk the talk if you want to see success. **WORK TO MAKE IT HAPPEN!**

NOTES

www.ingramcontent.com/pod-product-compliance
Lightning Source LLC
Chambersburg PA
CBHW070415190526
45169CB00003B/1261